God Can Do Anything!

WRITTEN BY MARY E. ERICKSON

ILLUSTRATED BY TERRY JULIEN

Chariot Books™
David C. Cook Publishing Co.

Chariot Books™ is an imprint of David C. Cook Publishing Co.
David C. Cook Publishing Co., Elgin, Illinois 60120
David C. Cook Publishing Co., Weston, Ontario
Nova Distribution Ltd., Newton Abbot, England

GOD CAN DO ANYTHING!
© 1993 by Mary Erickson for text and Terry Julien for illustrations

Designed by Terry Julien
First Printing, 1993
Printed in Singapore
97 96 95 94 93 5 4 3 2 1
Scripture quotations marked (NIV) are from the *Holy Bible, New International Version,*
© 1973, 1978, 1984, International Bible Society.
Used by permission of Zondervan Bible Publishers.

Library of Congress Cataloging-in-Publication Data
Erickson, Mary E.
God can do anything/by Mary Erickson
          p.   cm.
Summary: Uses seven Bible stories to demonstrate that God
can do many wonderful things, from healing the sick to giving eternal life.
ISBN 0-7814-0001-5
1. Providence and government of God--Juvenile literature.
2. God--Omnipotence--Juvenile literature. [1. God. 2. Bible stories.]
I. Title.
BT96.2.E75 1993
231'.5--dc20
                 92-33128
                 CIP

To my young readers

When my children were about your age, we sang a song together.

"Oh, who can make a flower?

I'm sure I can't. Can you?

Oh, who can make a flower?

No one but God. 'Tis true."

God made the world and everything in it. What are some other things God can do?

The Bible is full of stories that help us understand how good and powerful God is. In this book, you'll discover seven wonderful things God can do for people like you and me.

Dedicated with love to my daughters
Karen Lynn
and
Deborah Elmina

God Can Heal People

Praise the Lord, O my soul; and forget not all his benefits.
[He]. . . heals all your diseases.
Psalm 103:2, 3b

Naaman was an important man—a captain in the Syrian army. He and his wife and their little Hebrew slave girl lived happily together in a big, beautiful house.

One day the little slave saw her mistress crying. "Why are you sad?" she asked.

"My husband is sick with leprosy, and doctors cannot make him well."

"Don't worry," said the girl. "My God can heal him."

So Naaman traveled many miles to visit God's prophet Elisha in Samaria.

Elisha told Naaman, "Go to the Jordan River. Dip into it seven times, and you will be healed."

Straightening his shoulders and lifting his chin, Naaman said, "Me? Dip into that dirty water? Never!"

But his servants persuaded him to try it.

At the riverbank, Naaman took off his sword, helmet, and captain's cape. Stepping out of his sandals, he shuffled to the middle of the muddy river.

Quickly he dipped once. He came up sputtering and spitting and rubbing his eyes.

He looked at his arms. The white sores still covered his skin.

Pinching his nose and closing his eyes, he dipped again and again into the Jordan River.

When Naaman came up the seventh time, he looked at his arms. "Look!" he shouted. "The leprosy is gone. My skin is as pink and smooth as a baby's!"

Climbing into the chariot, Naaman and his servant galloped their horses to Samaria.

To thank Elisha, Naaman offered him gifts—silk robes and silver platters, gold coins and rare spices.

But Elisha shook his bald head. "I can't accept your gifts," he said. "I did nothing. You should give thanks to the living God who healed you."

(II Kings 5)

God can heal sick people . . . but sometimes He doesn't. I wonder if He allows sickness so people can learn important lessons or become a help to others.

God Can Feed the Hungry

Let them give thanks to the Lord . . . for he satisfies the thirsty and fills the hungry with good things.
Psalm 107:8a, 9

Elijah was a prophet. He had a special job, delivering messages for God.

One day Elijah told King Ahab, "It will not rain for three years because you and the people are wicked. You pray to idols made of wood and stone instead of to the Lord our God."

As the prophet left the angry king in the palace, God told him, "I'll take care of you. Hide in the ravine at Kerith. You can drink water from the brook, and I'll send you food."

I wonder how God will do that, thought Elijah. Strapping his pack on his back, he hiked to Kerith.

The next morning a raucous cry woke Elijah. Crawling out of his bedroll, he stumbled from the cave. A flock of black ravens flapped their wings and circled above him. "Cr-r-ruck! Cr-r-ruck!" they called, dropping bread and meat at the prophet's feet.

Elijah thanked God for the big birds that brought him food twice a day for many months.

One sunny morning Elijah got up and went to the brook to fill his water jug.

"Oh, no!" he groaned. "The brook is as dry as the desert. Now what will I do, God?"

"I have a plan," said God. "Pack up and go to Zarephath. A widow there will feed you. Give her this message: 'Your jar of flour will never be empty and the jug of oil will never run dry until I send rain.' "

So Elijah stayed in the widow's home. He ate bread at her table every day until rain fell and vegetable gardens grew green again.

(I Kings 17)

God can feed the hungry in many different ways. Sometimes He uses helpers like the ravens and the widow. I wonder how I can help God feed hungry people.

God Can Rescue from Danger

"Because he loves me," says the Lord, "I will rescue him."
Psalm 91:14

The prison was damp and dreary. Through a narrow window high on the dungeon wall, a moonbeam shone down on Peter sitting between two soldiers on a stone bench.

A strong soldier chained to Peter's right wrist said, "This is your last night."

"King Herod plans to kill you in the morning," added the young soldier chained to Peter's left wrist. "What did you do to make him so mad?"

Peter answered, "King Herod ordered me to stop talking about Jesus, but I couldn't. I must obey God rather than men."

"You escaped from prison once." The husky soldier rattled the chains. "But this time you won't get away."

Peter stretched his legs. "I'd better get some rest if I must stand trial tomorrow."

Leaning against the wall, Peter and his guards soon fell asleep.

Suddenly a light brighter than a flash of lightning filled the dungeon. An angel touched Peter on the shoulder and said, "Quickly now, get up!"

Peter sat up. The chains fell off his wrists, clanking on the stones. But the soldiers snored on.

"Put on your cloak and sandals," said the angel, "and follow me."

What a wonderful dream! thought Peter, following the angel down the prison pathway. They passed the first guard, who stood like a stone statue. They passed the second guard, who stared straight ahead.

When they reached the iron gate to the city, it swung open by itself. After they were safe inside the city walls, the angel disappeared.

The night breeze blew gently. Shivering, Peter pulled his cloak around him. "This is not a dream," he said. "Now I know the Lord sent His angel and rescued me from danger."

(Acts 12)

Because Satan tempts people to do evil things, I know I'll face trouble—sometime, someplace. But I'll remember how God rescued Peter. He is able to rescue me, too.

God Can Answer Prayer

"I prayed . . . and the Lord has granted me what I asked of him."
I Samuel 1:27

Hannah stared at the roast lamb and steaming vegetables.

"Why aren't you eating?" asked Elkanah, her husband.

"Other women have children," she said sadly. "I want a baby. I want a baby more than anything in this world."

The next day Hannah went to the temple. Kneeling, she sobbed and prayed, "Dear God, please give me a son. When he is old enough, I will give him back to You."

Eli, the priest, watched Hannah, but he couldn't hear her words. "You are acting very strange," he said. "Is something wrong?"

"I'm sad," Hannah said. "But I told God my problem."

Eli laid his hand on her head. "May God fill you with peace and answer your prayer."

And God did. A son was born to Hannah, and she named him Samuel. Hannah cuddled and nursed Samuel. She sang lullabies to him and told him about God.

When Samuel was old enough, Hannah packed his clothes and took him to the temple.

"Do you remember me?" she asked Eli. "Several years ago I prayed in this temple. I asked God for a son."

Samuel tugged on Eli's priestly robe. "My name is Samuel. I've come to live with you."

Hannah explained, "I promised I'd bring him back to be God's helper for the rest of his life."

The next year when Hannah visited the temple, she brought Samuel new clothes.

Eli praised the boy. "Samuel helps me in the temple every day," he said to Hannah. "Because you gave him to the Lord, I will ask God to give you many children."

And God did. Three more sons and two daughters filled Hannah's home with happy noises and her heart with love.

(I Samuel 1, 2)

When I pray and ask God for something, He always hears me. Sometimes He says, "Yes." Sometimes He says, "No." Sometimes He says, "Wait!" God is wise. He knows what's best for me.

God Can Solve Problems

"I am the Lord, the God of all mankind. Is anything too hard for me?"
Jeremiah 32:27

Captain Gideon stood on a hill in the moonlight. Tents and camels of the Midianites filled the valley like sand on the sea-shore.

"Dear God," Gideon prayed. "You want me to attack that Midianite army of 135,000 soldiers. How can I win with only 300 men?"

"I have already solved the problem," God answered. "Take your servant Purah and go to the camp of Midian. Listen to what their soldiers are saying."

Gideon and Purah crept down the hill, hiding in the shadows of trees. They crawled through deep grass. Crouching behind a tent, they listened.

"I had a strange dream," they heard one man say. "A round loaf of barley bread tumbled down the hill. The loaf crashed into our tent, flipped it over, and knocked it flat."

"I know what that means," said a man with a quivering voice. "The bread stands for the army of Gideon. The tent stands for the army of Midian. Gideon's God will help them destroy us."

Gideon hurried back to camp. He called to his troops, "Wake up! We're going to attack the Midianites tonight."

Gideon gave each man a trumpet and a clay jar with a torch inside. "Surround the Midianite camp!" he ordered.

At a signal from Gideon, 300 Israelites blew their trumpets. The sound rumbled like thunder through the valley.

They smashed the clay jars, filling the air with a terrible crash. Flames leaped from the torches. A circle of fire lit the sky. Then the soldiers shouted, "A sword for the Lord and for Gideon!"

The Midianites stumbled from their tents. Swinging their swords in the darkness, they killed one another in their confusion.

What a victory God gave Gideon and his army that night!

(*Judges 7*)

Sometimes I have problems that seem big to me, but I know that nothing is too hard for God. I'll remember Gideon and his small army, and I'll trust God to help me solve my problems, too.

God Can Go Anywhere

"For the Lord your God will be with you wherever you go."
Joshua 1:9

Three young Hebrew men stood in the palace in Babylon.

"Is it true," asked King Nebuchadnezzar, "that you three did not worship the golden image I made?"

"Yes, it's true," said Shadrach.

Stomping down his throne steps, the king said, "In my kingdom, you worship my idols. I'll give you one more chance. My musicians will play again so you can bow to my golden image."

The young men shook their heads.

Meshach said, "We bow only to the true God."

The king's jaw stiffened. "If you refuse to obey, I'll throw you into a roaring fire. Then who will be able to rescue you?"

Abednego said, "Our God can."

"But even if He does not, " Shadrach added, "we want you to know that we would never worship any golden idol."

The king's face turned red. "Guards!" he shouted. "Put more wood on the fire. Make that furnace seven times hotter than it's ever been before."

Tying the young men with heavy ropes, strong soldiers carried

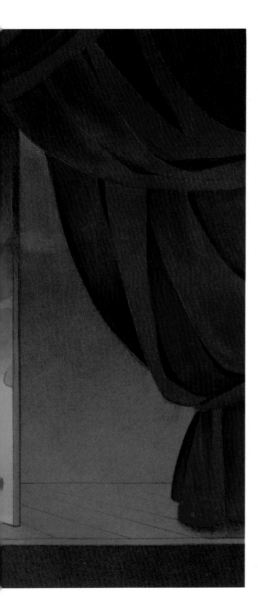

them into the furnace room. The king and his governors followed.

The soldiers opened the furnace door and threw the three men into the fire. The fire was so hot that flames leaped out and killed the soldiers.

The king stood back, watching through the open door. "Look!" he gasped. "I see men walking about. And there are four of them! One shines brighter than gold. He looks like a god."

Then the king shouted, "Shadrach! Meshach! Abednego! Come out!"

The three young Hebrews stepped out of the furnace. Their hair was not singed. Their skin was not burned. Their clothes didn't smell smoky.

"Your God was with you in the fire," the king said, amazed at what he had seen. "I admit it. No other god can do what your God does."

(Daniel 3)

If God can go into a fiery furnace, I know He can go with me anywhere. He promised He would.

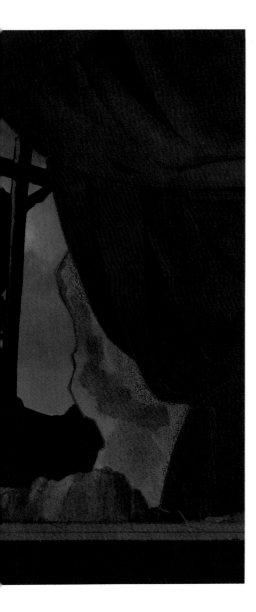

God Can Give Life

"They killed him by hanging him on a tree, but God raised him from the dead."
Acts 10:39b, 40a

At nine o'clock in the morning, a noisy crowd gathered on a hill outside Jerusalem.

Thud! Thud! Swinging heavy hammers, soldiers nailed Jesus' hands and feet to a wooden cross.

"Jesus is good and kind. Why are they crucifying him?" a woman asked.

"Because He told lies," someone sneered. "He said He's the Son of God."

At three o'clock a great earthquake shook the ground. Rocks split in half. People screamed and ran away.

With one last loud cry, Jesus died.

A kind man named Joseph of Arimathea and his friend took the body of Jesus to a nearby garden. Some women who loved Jesus followed.

The two friends wrapped Jesus in soft white cloths and placed Him in a tomb carved in a rock. Grunting and pushing, they rolled a huge stone into the entrance.

Early Sunday morning, several women hurried to the tomb

with spices and perfume to put on Jesus' body.

"But how will we get into the tomb?" one woman asked. "Who will move that huge stone for us?"

"No need to worry!" shouted the first one to enter the garden. "The stone has been rolled away."

The women rushed inside the rock tomb. Sitting on a stone ledge was an angel in white, surrounded by a dazzling light.

"Don't be afraid," the angel said. "I know you're looking for Jesus. But He's not here."

"Look!" gasped one woman. "The soft cloths that were wrapped around his head have been neatly folded."

"Who took him away?" cried another.

"No one," the angel answered. "God brought Jesus back to life. Go tell your friends that Jesus is living again."

(Mark 15, 16)

I feel sad when people die. Sometimes I cry. But now I know God is more powerful than death. Someday God will make us live again, just as He did Jesus. We'll go to heaven and live with Him forever.

Ah, Sovereign Lord,
you have made the heavens and the earth
by your great power and outstretched arm.
Nothing is too hard for you.

Jeremiah 32:17